The Scie

MW01284405

Discipline:

Controlling Your Thoughts, Develop Self Confidence and Developing Mental Toughness to Achieve Your Goals

About the Author

Quawsi Samuel is a proud and savvy investment portfolio manager, Author and medical and financial Underwriter. After receiving a Bachelors of Science at Sunderland University, Quawsi now works for a medium sized financial company in the Caribbean Islands with an asset base of 1.5 Billion USD in which he engages in Medical, financial and economical risk assessment and at the same time manages his personal investment portfolio business. He aspires to be an internationally recognized author, motivational speaker on various topic such as goal setting and achievement, Investments, finances and risk assessment. Quawsi firmly believes that the future will be in desperate need of proper financial, Economic and goal plan setting education as a result of the globalized economy we now live in. In his spare time,he loves spending time with his lovely wife and family , enjoys technically analyzing the forex, stocks, cryptocurrencies, commodities and the futures market and takes pleasure in reading a well crafted book in a variety of different genres.

Table of Contents

Introduction

I would like to thank you for purchasing the book *"The Science of Self-disciple: Controlling Your Thoughts, Develop Self-confidence, and developing Mental Toughness to Achieve Your Goals."*

Imagine if you could be resilient, have brilliant clarity in your thoughts, and daily focus on realizing your goals by consistently achieving one after the other. More often than not, people and their minds don't work as a team. Wouldn't it be wonderful if you could develop a mindset that allows you to make the most of the opportunities you have? Your quality of life depends on the way you think or perceive things, and the manner in which you deal with the external world and your internal feelings. By merely tweaking your perception a little, you can achieve surprisingly pleasant results. At times, it might feel like, regardless of what you do, obstacles are blocking your path everywhere. External factors may also apply, but largely, obstacles happen through our own perceptions. All those who consistently overcome all the obstacles that they face are the ones who become successful in life.

Laser-sharp focus, resilience and the ability to keep going even when others would have quit are the essentials to achieving success. In this book, you will learn about self-discipline, steps for developing self-discipline, understanding and learning resilience, controlling your thoughts and developing self-confidence. By developing these habits, you will be closer to achieving your goals than you ever were before. So, let us get started without further ado.

Chapter One: About Self-discipline

We all have different dreams and aspirations. However, how many of us have the genuine passion and focus necessary for keeping that dream alive and for making it come true? Well, more often than not, not many of us can do so. Perhaps your motivation fizzles out once you start the task or something else along the way distracts you. Do you feel that you don't have the necessary self-discipline to let go of your harmful habits? Or have you started working on including a positive habit earlier, and then after a while, you just gave up on it altogether?

If your answer is yes for any of the above questions, then you have just proved that you are human, just like the significant chunk of the population who keep thinking, dreaming and fantasizing about all the things that they want to do "someday." However, that "someday" just stays elusive and they never get any of those things done. Instead, they try to procrastinate or come up with excuses for not doing that job. Regardless of what you are trying to do, the one thing that's necessary is self-discipline. Without self-discipline, you will never get anything done. It could be anything like losing weight, studying for an exam, starting your business venture, getting a good grade, quitting drinking or smoking, or pretty much anything else that you can think of.

If you think of success as a car, then self-discipline is its engine. Regardless of how powerful and sophisticated your vehicle might be, without the engine, it won't get you anywhere. Likewise, it doesn't matter how inspiring or amazing your goals are, without self-discipline, they will just remain as goals or dreams. If you want to reach your destination, then you need self-discipline to help you on the way.

A successful businessman named Herbert Grey carried out a study for eleven years to find the common denominator of success. At the end of his research and study, he concluded that self-discipline is the common denominator necessary for achieving success. If you want to attain something in your life, then you need to let go of all the harmful mental negligence like giving excuses, blaming others for your action or lack of it, justifying your passive behavior and procrastinating and should instead strive to develop self-discipline. Self-discipline is the ability to do something that you should be doing and when you should be doing it, regardless of whether you want to or not. Self-discipline is the key to success, and the lack of it makes you feel frustrated in life.

There is just a small difference between where you are in life right now, and the result that you want to achieve, and this difference is a habit. In other words, you are always just a simple habit away from attaining your desired results. Human beings are creatures of habit, but not of discipline. We unknowingly form patterns and stick to them, but we don't gravitate towards discipline. Discipline needs self-control and determination. John Maxwell had once said, "Most people want to avoid pain, and discipline is usually painful," that's the reason why the lack of self-discipline is considered to be the most straightforward formula for failure. If you want to try to incorporate a positive habit, then you need discipline. A significant level of discipline indeed produces good habits. Even though human beings are a creature of habit (all that we habitually do decides the course of our lives), to make your life count, you will have to force yourself to not just concentrate on things that are easy and fun, but start doing all such things that might be difficult but are necessary. Only when you do this, will you be able to reach your goals and achieve all the greatness and success you have always dreamed of.

It is easier to form a dangerous habit than to develop a good one. Well, we all tend to gravitate towards harmful practices to cope with any emotional or psychological challenges in life. Harmful habits like drinking, smoking, substance abuse and all other addictions can become coping mechanisms quite easily. Harmful habits can quickly turn into addictions, and people make use of them as a veil to hide behind when life gets difficult. Some people tend to make use of these destructive habits to express their hatred towards themselves, and this is quite unfortunate. All the emotional traumas a person might have suffered in the past will make him or her feel worthless, undeserving and incapable of achieving anything good in life.

Well, that's enough talk about doom and gloom. The good news is that if you can form harmful habits, then you are capable of overcoming them and develop the self-discipline that will help you to grow in life. Self-discipline can assist you in improving your level of self-confidence, happiness, productivity, sense of accomplishment, to name a few. If you feel like you aren't able to do it alone, then reach out for help. You are never alone unless you believe this to be so.

Rome wasn't built in a day, and you cannot learn self-discipline overnight. It takes a lot of conscious effort, persistence and patience. These are the building blocks of self-discipline. When you learn to discipline yourself to put in the necessary hard work, stay resilient, and endure while doing things that you should be doing, then you will start liking yourself and even accepting yourself. All this will make you stronger and more confident and help to improve your self-image as well. If you are convinced about how important self-discipline is, read on to learn about the seven simple steps that you should follow for developing this unusual trait.

The importance of positive messages

Your mind creates the world that you live in and where the battle of life is fought. Therefore, you should be careful about what you feed it. Make sure that you are feeding it with some positive messages that are inspiring and motivating. The way you are is greatly influenced by all that you read and hear about regularly. So, stop wasting your time reading pointless books, watching unhelpful series or videos that will just enhance your lack of self-discipline. It is okay to do these things once in a while, but not regularly. Anything that isn't actively helping you to work towards achieving your goals is just a wastage of your time and attention. This, in turn, weakens your resilience necessary for being successful. You can change the course of your life by changing the way you think. You can change the way you think by feeding your mind content that's motivating an inspiring. There are a couple of subtle changes that take place when your mind is exposed to the motivational content. Your self-esteem will improve, and this will make you feel better about yourself. By removing all doubts and overcoming any inferiority complexes, you will feel better. It will provide you with the necessary courage to overcome your fears, and when you overcome your fears, you will be a step closer to achieving your dreams. Positive messages and reinforcements will provide you with the strength required to take the first step towards achieving your goals. Your strength, courage and determination can be improved with positive reinforcement.

Surround yourself with positive people

If all those around you lack self-discipline, even you will struggle with incorporating this trait. The company you keep shapes your personality. So, if you are looking for ways in which you can improve your self-discipline, then you should think about surrounding yourself with people who are confident, goal-oriented, result oriented, focused and full of integrity. Try surrounding yourself with like-minded people or those who have gone through a similar phase you are going through. All their positivity is bound to rub off on you, and you are bound to gain something useful from it. It will help to create an "if they can, so can I" attitude. Creating an atmosphere that is conducive to growth and development is essential if you want to achieve your goals.

A strong reason

Think about the reasons why you want the goal you desire and then think about how badly you want it. If your idea of achieving a specific goal is active, then you will automatically find the necessary strength to create a path to it as well. For instance, if you want to stop smoking and your reason is to be alive long enough to watch your children settle down in life, then it will provide you with the necessary strength to keep going as well. Your will to do something should be so high that you automatically find the power required to keep going. When you want to do something, and you want to do it wholeheartedly, you will always be able to find a way of accomplishing it.

Visualization

You cannot actualize anything that you aren't capable of visualizing. Everything great that anyone has ever achieved always starts with imagination. Look around and think about everything you see. All that you can see was first conceptualized and visualized by someone and then executed. Therefore, start imagining your goal if you want to achieve it. In this case, you aim to develop self-discipline. So, begin by visualizing that you already have good self-discipline and all the other necessary habits for achieving your goals.

Try to make your imagination as vivid as you possibly can and visualize that you have already reached your goals. Think about how you will feel once you have achieved your goals and how your life will be. Your thoughts can influence your personality, and they can shape your life. Therefore, stop looking at yourself the way you are right now and instead will yourself to become the person that you want to be. You can achieve whatever your mind is capable of conceiving and believing. Only when you can think something, will you be able to find the necessary motivation to make it.

Setting goals

Your mind is always goal-oriented, and it contains a success mechanism that you can unlock by setting goals that are attainable and measurable. So, you should start with setting goals for yourself. The first step is to set small goals or if you are setting a big goal, make sure that it can be broken down into several more modest goals. Not just that, your goals should be achievable and measurable. For instance, if you want to start writing a book, a small goal that you can set for yourself is to start writing short stories once a week. Make sure that it is at least 500 words or so and keep it simple. Do this for a while, and all your short stories will condition your mind to reprogram itself, redefine yourself as someone who isn't a quitter. When you start enjoying the joy of completing a task, you will feel better. When your mind has reprogrammed itself and has formed the positive association with writing, your level of confidence will increase, and you can start setting bigger goals for yourself.

Being accountable

A perfect way in which you can improve your self-discipline is by making yourself accountable to somebody else. Keep telling someone about the goals you want to achieve and ask them to check on your progress. When you do this, you automatically make yourself goal-oriented. You are not just accountable to yourself, but to someone else as well. You will notice that you will become resilient and will keep doing things that will enhance your self-discipline because you want to stay consistent with something you have said that you would do. When you commit to someone else, even when you are low on motivation, the idea of the commitment you've made will keep you going. You can choose a friend, your partner, or even a family member for this. It will undoubtedly make you feel better when you realize that you have kept your word.

Start taking action

If you want to transform your dream into reality, then you will need to take action. Your efforts should be consistent and relevant. Do things that will help you to achieve your goals. Once you have followed all the steps that have been discussed above, you should start working on them as well. Make a note of the things you want to do and your reasons for it as well. Create a plan of action that will make you take small actionable steps on a daily basis to work towards your goal. You should remember that it might be a little hard initially. However, once you have formed a habit, it does get easier. You need courage to achieve success. Courage is necessary for not just starting but to keep going even in the face of adversities. It is essential not to give up when things don't turn out like you thought they would. Psychologists often say that it takes three to four weeks of consistent and relevant actions to form a habit. Once you start achieving the daily goals you have set for yourself, you will not feel like stopping after that. When this happens, you will have successfully formed a positive habit. In the words of Ralph Waldo Emerson "He who is not every day conquering some fear has not learned the secret of life." Start taking steps today, and you can turn your life around and transform it into something that you have always wanted.

Chapter Two: How To Become Relentless

Do you want more out of life than an average person? Do you want to be relentless while pursuing a goal? Do you want to live the life that you always wanted to? If yes, then you need to work on developing the ability to be relentless. A persistent person will keep going even when others would have given up.

At times, it might feel like a never-ending uphill battle when you are trying to fulfill your dreams. The key is to keep working on small goals, and all the victories that come your way will motivate you to keep going towards the next task on the list. If you want to win in life, you should become relentless.

Did you ever wonder why so many things that we start never reach a logical conclusion? It is because we aren't pursuing them relentlessly. What exactly does it mean to pursue a dream or anything else relentlessly? It says that you shouldn't give up even when things get hard, boring or stale. Even when you are passionate about something, after a while, they do get tiresome. It means that you should start facing all the inevitable obstacles that come your way without giving up on your dream. Change isn't easy, but if you want to grow then change is inevitable.

It means being patient and consistently doing things that will help you to achieve your goals. Finally, it means to keep pursuing your goal even when others don't understand what you are doing. Some might think that your goal is crazy or maybe not worth your while. However, that is their opinion, and they don't know what you want. Relentless pursuit might make others uncomfortable but that doesn't mean you should stop doing what you are doing. How do you know that relentless effort can work in your favor? There are biblical stories of people who overcame tremendous obstacles to do something they believed in even when the whole world didn't believe them. Ordinary people like Rudy Ruettiger and Erin Brockovich kept pursuing their beliefs tirelessly, and that's what helped them in becoming successful. Persistence and resilience are the differentiating factors between ordinary and extraordinary individuals.

What are your goals? Do you want to start your own business, start a charitable organization, or mint a lot of money? Regardless of what your dreams are, when you become relentless, you will find the passion and confidence necessary to face any challenges and overcome them as well. You will get what you want if you can pursue it without giving up.

If you want to be the best, then you should work on engineering your life in such a manner that you don't stop until you have achieved what you wanted and then you keep going until you have completed what is next. Once you have done that, you will keep going back for more. That is what being relentless means.

There are some who feel a spark when they hear the word relentless, and then there are those who can't think of anything beyond pain and defeat when they listen to the same word. Good or bad, being relentless should be a part of your character if you want to become great. Being harsh means not giving up until you get what you wanted, but it also means disregarding all the negative consequences until you attain the desired results.

For instance, all the great NBA players like Michael Jordan and Kobe Bryant worked hard, listened to the advice given to them, and kept pushing themselves. They weren't content with just one championship ring and kept on working hard until their hands were covered with them. They didn't stop working hard, were patient, and that's how they became unstoppable. You shouldn't settle for good or great if you want to be relentless. The aim is to become invincible and not settle for anything less than that. The thing is, anyone can become relentless. However, there are only a few people who can stay in the game long enough to attain the results they desire. Initially, when everything is shiny and new, things are exciting. The key is to keep going when the novelty fades away. In this section, you will learn about three simple steps that will help you in becoming unstoppable while chasing your dreams.

Doing the work

You needn't love the job, but you should do it, and enjoy the results you achieve as well. You should work hard, even if it means burning the midnight oil or waking up at the crack of dawn to do things that you want. It doesn't sound complicated, does it? You should do the work, put in all the necessary time and effort until you get there. At times, it means doing things that you don't want in order to get what you want. It might be quite challenging, especially when that little voice in your head keeps telling you to focus on short-term rewards. Short-term rewards might seem quite tempting, but they fade away when compared to long-term results you are trying to achieve. It is about going for the long-term win and about being great. Being relentless means putting in more effort even when you feel like giving up and it requires a lot of hard work.

Start being obsessive

The one question that you should think about is, "what is your goal for which you are willing to give it your all?" Well, you certainly cannot give your all for everything. You need to know what your priorities are and how hard you are willing to work towards reaching the greatness that you want. What is the one thing that you want to be the best at? Take some time and think about it. You can be good at multiple things, but what is the one thing that you want to be the best at? Once you know what it is, you need to be obsessed with that one thing. Pick that one area in your life that is your top priority and on which you want to spend most of your time. When you know this answer, hone your passion in such a manner that it becomes an obsession for you. When this happens, you will start learning everything you can about it and doing all the right things that will help you along the way.

Be comfortable with yourself

Have you ever heard the age-old adage "it is lonely at the top?" Well, it is true. When you become resilient and relentless, you may not have a lot of time to socialize, and you should be okay with it. Learn to make peace with yourself and be comfortable with yourself. You need to spend a lot of time by yourself when you are working on your dreams. It is okay to do that, and it is okay to have a small circle of friends. You shouldn't depend on anyone else for the support you need, and you should learn to keep going.

So, do you think you are relentless? Do you want to be relentless? If your answer is yes, then you need to start putting in all the time and effort, get obsessive about that one thing, and become comfortable with yourself. We all have the potential to become relentless. Don't let comfort get in your way or make discomfort discourage you.

Chapter Three: How to Develop Self-Confidence

We often admire those who are confident and seem to inspire confidence in others as well. A self-confident person knows how to face their fears and is a natural risk taker. They know that regardless of all the obstacles that they face, they have what it takes to overcome those troubles. Self-confident people can maintain a positive outlook towards life even when things don't work in their favor. Wouldn't it be brilliant if you could possess this sort of self-confidence, all year long? Guess what? You can do that. In this chapter, you will learn about self-esteem and how you can improve your confidence quotient. You need to understand that self-confidence like any other life skill can be acquired. It all boils down to a straightforward question: How can you expect others to believe in you if you don't believe in yourself?

There are some simple tips discussed below. You shouldn't just read and then forget about them. You should start consciously practicing these tips daily, and after a while, your confidence levels will increase. With some time, practice, and patience, you can become self-confident.

Steer clear of all negativity

Take some time and evaluate your inner circle. The company you keep influences your general mindset without any conscious thought. It is quite difficult to do this, but it is high time that you get away from those who put you down and destroy your self-confidence. Even a temporary break from all the negative people in your life can have a positive impact on your life. Maintain a positive mindset even when you don't feel positive about how things are going on. Project your positive attitude into your daily interactions and always hit the ground running. Be excited about the things that you are doing and stop thinking about all the problems or things that aren't going right in your life. If you keep overthinking about everything that is going wrong, you will never find any mental peace. Try thinking of solutions for your problems instead of letting them trouble you.

Changing your body language

The way you talk, your posture, your smile, and the eye contact you maintain are all critical. Your body language speaks volumes about your self-confidence. The simple act of standing with your back straight and your shoulders back gives others the impression that you are quite confident. Smiling will not only make you feel relaxed, but it is quite contagious as well. When you smile, you are automatically making others feel comfortable as well. A good posture and a bright smile will make you seem happy and confident. Communication is so much more than just the words you say, and it is of two types; verbal communication and non-verbal communication. The non-verbal interface is made up of your body language. Subtle gestures like maintaining eye contact while talking instead of looking at your feet will make you seem confident. Speak slowly and clearly. If you are always in a rush to get the words out of your mouth, you look sloppy and anxious. Not only will you seem self-assured, but also others will be able to understand what you are saying. Pay extra attention to the way you dress, the style of your hair and keep yourself well groomed. When you do this, you are automatically improving your body image too. Your clothes convey a lot about you, and when you are dressed smartly, you seem confident. So, start paying attention to the way you dress.

Do not accept failure

When you are chasing success, you are bound to fail a couple of times. The important thing is that you should never allow failure to stop you and you should never give up. It is okay to fail, learn from your mistakes, and move on. Dwelling on your failures will not do you any good, and it will prevent you from going forward. Regardless of how complicated and impossible a problem might seem, there is always a solution. It is all about how hard you try to overcome the obstacle and when you do overcome an obstacle, your self-confidence grows too. All the negative thoughts that are consistently present in your mind will just lower your confidence. If you keep putting yourself down, and keep telling yourself that you aren't good enough, you never will be. You need to work on building your self-confidence and developing a positive body image. Your thoughts dictate the way you act and the way you act defines your life. So, the next time you are in a self-critical mode, be mindful of all the negative things you are telling yourself. Engage in positive self-talk instead and pep yourself with positive affirmations. Keep telling yourself that you can do anything and you will be able to do it eventually, if not immediately.

Always be prepared

Always be well prepared. If you are working on a project, then make sure that you have done plenty of research and you know what to expect. Be prepared for the likely obstacles that you might run into, a way to overcome them and, if possible, think of a way to avoid them altogether as well. When you are well prepared, you will not be caught off-guard. When you aren't caught off guard, you will be able to do better in life.

A great list

Life is peppered with challenges, and when things become difficult, it is essential to keep up your self-confidence. Take some time out, and make a list of all the things in your life that you are grateful for. Not just that - make a list of accomplishments that you are proud of as well. Once you have made these records, stick it in a place with excellent visibility like on your refrigerator door or the mirror of your dresser. Keep glancing at that list whenever you feel like your self-worth is taking a blow. It will act as a reminder of all the things that you are capable of doing, and you will feel better about yourself. You don't have to look for inspiration or motivation from any external factor, and you are in fact, your source of motivation.

Preparing for the journey ahead

So, how can you build self-confidence correctly without crossing over into the territory of arrogance? There is no quick fix for developing confidence. The good news is that with a little bit of patience and hard work, you can become quite confident. Self-confidence will help you to achieve success. There are three steps that you should take on your journey to becoming a confident person. Let us take a look at these three levels.

The first step is to prep yourself for your journey towards becoming a confident person. Take stock of where you are in life, the journey you have been on so far and the destination you are headed towards, forming the right mindset for the journey, and then committing to staying on track. Think about how far you have come in life and all the things you have achieved. Make an achievement log and list down ten things that you have accomplished so far in your life. Place this list on your desk or anywhere else where it is plainly visible to you.

Use the SWOT analysis for understanding your strengths and weaknesses. You can seek the help of others to do this. You might not realize specific strengths or weaknesses you might have, and others can help by giving you a better perspective. For a couple of minutes thinking about all the opportunities and threats that you might face. Reflect on your strengths and think of ways in which you can hone them.

Think about all those things that are important to you and the direction you are headed in life. You should start setting goals for yourself in this step. Goals can help to provide you with a sense of direction and also assist in measuring all the good that you have achieved, the distance you have come, and the road that lies ahead. You can set specific short-term and long-term goals for yourself. You can also set goals for different aspects of your life. If you have any significant goals, then try breaking them down into simpler and smaller goals that are readily achievable.

Don't forget to celebrate your victories, regardless of how big or small they might be. Once you have done all this, you should start managing your mind. Learn to let go of all the negative self-talk and criticisms. Instead, you should focus on repeating a couple of positive affirmations daily. Positive self-talk can do wonders for your self-confidence. You can make use of mental imagery and visualization to improve your levels of confidence. Think about how amazing you will feel when you achieve your goals, and this will make even the most difficult of your goals seem quite achievable. The final step is to make a commitment to yourself about attaining your goals. You need to make this commitment and stick to it as no one else can do this for you.

Chapter Four: Developing Mental Toughness for Achieving Goals

Mental toughness is about developing a mindset that will enable you to work tirelessly and resolutely on something regardless of all the obstacles that stand in your way. It is about being resilient even when the odds aren't in your favor. A mentally tough person will have a "where there is a will, there is a way" attitude towards anything in life. They have the internal motivation and the will to keep going even in decidedly tricky situations and circumstances. If you know what your passion is, the next step is to keep going until you have reached your destination. It is about working out all the glitches you face and succeeding in spite of all that. You cannot be mentally tough if you are someone who gets discouraged quite quickly by all the obstacles you face, mistakes you make, and the criticism you receive. Similarly, you cannot become tough if you are quickly bogged down by anxiety, frustrations, stress or fears.

Mental toughness is the term that is used for describing a mind frame that helps people to achieve their goals. It is a non-excuse attitude that helps in developing the mindset of a winner. Well, now that you know what mental toughness is all about, the next step is to become mentally tough. In this section, you will learn about the different ways in which you can become mentally tough.

Identification of challenges and establishing goals

Being mentally healthy or strong means that you are capable of adapting yourself to stressful situations or trauma without breaking down. Resilience isn't a characteristic that a person is born with and it is a process that anyone can learn and develop. Being emotionally tough doesn't mean that you aren't capable of feeling or experiencing any negative emotion or pain. Emotional resilience is always improved in the face of adversity - a painful situation to bounce back from. What does it mean to "bounce back" from such circumstances or experiences? To develop your emotional resilience, you should be willing to work on improving specific essential skills like the ability of planning and executing your plans, building confidence, self-awareness, managing strong impulses and the ability to communicate effectively and to solve problems efficiently.

If you want to become mentally strong, then you need to learn to manage your feelings. You certainly cannot control what life throws at you, but you can control the way you react to it. You are always in control of your reactions. It isn't an innate quality, and you need to learn to manage your emotions productively. You will learn more about managing and developing certain desirable traits in the coming chapters.

Is there anything you would like to change about yourself? Before you can start developing your emotional and mental strength, you should take a while and think about all your strengths, weaknesses and the challenges that you will need to overcome. Think about all those aspects of your life that you would like to change. Make a list of these things and see how it will help you to achieve your goals. For instance, if one of the challenges that you want to overcome is the difficulty in asserting your needs and you want to fix this issue. Then your immediate goal should be to stop being indecisive and become more assertive. It isn't just about identifying all those areas that you should work on but about celebrating your strengths as well. List down all your positive traits and characteristics. Read through them and celebrate yourself! These favorable attributes will come in handy while achieving your goals.

It might sound old fashioned, but maintaining a journal will undoubtedly help you. Keeping a journal can assist you to understand what you might be feeling, the experiences that created such emotions, and it helps in letting go of unnecessary stress as well. It is quite easy to maintain a journal. Just set aside 20 minutes daily for writing about your day. You can write about how you are feeling, your thoughts or anything else. Write about the incidents that bothered you and the emotions you felt. Think about the reasons for such feelings and make a note of it as well. Just write down everything that you think! It doesn't necessarily have to be good or bad. Your journal is the perfect outlet for all the emotions you might be feeling.

At times, it might be difficult to figure things out on your own, and you might need a little additional help. If you feel that you are struggling to determine what you are feeling, then consider talking to a therapist or a counselor. There is no shame in accepting that you need some help. It is entirely reasonable to seek help and don't let anyone else tell you otherwise. Your aim should be to become mentally tough and to do that you will need to overcome all the unresolved issues that you might be dealing with knowingly or unknowingly.

Staying even-keeled

If you are trying to cope with any negative emotions by warming up to different vices like drugs, alcohol or anything destructive, then stop doing that immediately. Stop trying to internalize the negative feelings you feel. If you want to become mentally tough, the first step is to take into consideration all those negative emotions that hinder your performance and productivity. The next time you feel stressed, don't reach for your pack of cigarettes. Instead, think of the reason that is causing you stress and see what you can do about such a thing. Start taking steps to push these vices away from your life. They indeed shouldn't determine how you feel or control the way you act.

You need to take care of yourself. Maintain a healthy diet, exercise regularly, and give yourself some time for resting and relaxing. It will help in making you feel mentally stronger. By taking good care of your body, you are developing your sense of wellbeing. Your mind will be more relaxed. Start exercising daily for at least 30 minutes. If you cannot do it daily, then do it every alternate day at least. You don't necessarily have to go to the gym to exercise. You can swim, play a sport you like, go for a jog, do some yoga or any other activity that will get your blood pumping. Start eating a healthy and a balanced diet that consists of whole foods, lean proteins, healthy fats and seasonal fruit and vegetables. A healthy diet will make you feel good about yourself. It is essential that you sleep for at least 7 hours every night. Always keep your body thoroughly hydrated and have at least eight glasses of water per day.

Keep challenging and opening yourself up to learning all the time. Over a period, you will keep accruing knowledge and, as a result, you will become mentally tougher and wiser. Don't get stuck in a mental or a physical rut. Learn to be curious and well informed about the world. Be a sponge and absorb information. Start reading books, watch good and informative movies, attend concerts and plays, go to the ballet, and start taking an interest in some form of art or the other.

You can derive strength from paying some attention to your spiritual side as well. Having a connection with and doing something that's greater than yourself can provide you with a sense of purpose and make you feel stronger from within. Get in touch with your spirituality, and you will be able to find some peace. It doesn't mean that you have to spend hours on end meditating or anything of that sort. Just take some time out and go to a place of worship, meditate for 15 minutes, or go for a walk and admire nature. Do anything that makes you feel closer to the cosmos.

Developing mental and emotional strength

You can start developing your mental strength by setting reasonable goals for yourself. It is not just about setting goals, but it is about taking the necessary steps to achieve your goals as well. If you want to start working towards your goals, you will need to start applying yourself. It means that you will have to ask yourself even when you are bored or going through some turmoil, and sticking to the plan until you have accomplished the goals you have set for yourself. It will not be an easy feat and don't let it scare you. Practice makes a man perfect, and this age-old adage is true! Keep practicing, and you will get better! If you have set some big goals for yourself and they seem impossible, try breaking them down into manageable steps that are doable. For instance, if you want to become assertive, then your first step should be to learn to speak up for yourself at least three times every week. These instances could be major or minor ones. But you will have to speak up for yourself. Develop a "stick with it" mindset. Even if you face an obstacle or a setback, keep trying and don't give up. Start being resilient and don't worry about the troubles you come across. The goal is to keep going until you have achieved what you wanted to do. Think of all the failures as an opportunity to learn and please do learn from them. Every day is a new day and don't let the troubles from your past sneak up on you.

Negativity can sneak up on you quite quickly. It can be stemmed from a negative emotion that you are harboring within yourself or it could be because of something external to negative feedback or toxic people around you. While certain things are beyond your control, the one thing that you can control is the way you feel about yourself and your life. Don't let any negativity live within you. You cannot control what others think about you, but you can certainly control the way you feel about yourself. There are different ways in which you can manage all the negativity. You can start by identifying and challenging such negative thoughts. You can reduce your interaction with harmful and toxic people. If you think you are in a toxic relationship, learn to break free from it. Don't entertain negativity in any form.

Make use of positive self-talk to build up your mental strength. Making use of positive affirmations will help you in developing a positive outlook while getting rid of all negativity around you. Take a couple of minutes and look at yourself in the mirror and say something positive and motivating to yourself. You can tell something that you believe in or something that you would like to be true to yourself.

When you learn to control your emotions instead of letting them control you, you are giving yourself an opportunity to weigh your options before deciding on a particular choice. Take a minute, count to ten, before you let a negative emotion boil over. It might sound like a cliché, but it does work. Before having an emotional reaction towards something, take a moment to gather your thoughts and react accordingly. You can try practicing meditation as well, and it can help you to maintain your calm. Meditation can help you to stay objective while providing you with the necessary time for making sense of your thoughts and emotions. Instead of reacting immediately, you can weigh your thoughts and emotions and then think of your next step.

If you are always sensitive to the petty annoyances and verbal barbs or taunts that we all tend to come across daily, then you will end up becoming quite bitter. Also, you will be wasting a lot of your precious time and energy thinking about unnecessary things, which don't matter at the end of the day. When you start spending time thinking about all such things and start paying attention to them, you are making them a significant problem that will increase your stress. Learning to adjust your attitude can help you to let these petty and trivial issues go without increasing your level of stress. You are not only preventing the wastage of your valuable time and energy, but you are also saving yourself the trouble of having to deal with extra stress. Instead of stressing yourself out about all these things, you should develop a healthy routine of thinking about the things that are bothering you, then take a deep breath, calm yourself down, and once you are calm, think of the best way in which you can deal with that issue.

For instance, if your spouse keeps forgetting to put the cap on the tube of toothpaste after using it, you should understand that such a thing isn't as important to your partner as it is to you. If this bothers you, think about all the other things that your partner does for you that make you feel good and in comparison, you can certainly let this small flaw of theirs go. Don't try to be a perfectionist, at least not all the time. When you do this, you are setting high expectations for yourself, and these tend to be entirely unrealistic. Try to be realistic while thinking about things and don't let the idea of perfection create any additional stress or burden. You can make use of a straightforward visualization exercise that will help you to let go of little things that seem to be bothering you. Take a small stone or pebble and hold it in your hand. Transfer all your negative thoughts that are bothering you into that pebble. And once you are ready, swing it as hard as you can or toss it into a pond. Visualize that all the petty problems are drowning along with the pebble that's sinking. You are casting away all your negative emotions.

We tend to get so caught up in our problems that we tend to look at things from a different perspective. A fresh attitude towards existing troubles can help in solving your problems. If you feel like you have hit a dead end with something, take a break and relax. Once you feel refreshed, start thinking of ways in which you can tackle that problem. If you change the way in which you are approaching a problem, you might find a solution to it in no time. Here are a couple of different things that you can try to get a new perspective on things.

Start reading. Reading the daily news or a book can help you to step into someone else's world, and this serves as a good reminder to let you know that the world is a vast place and that your problems are nothing significant when you think about the entirety of the universe we live in.

All those who are mentally as well as emotionally strong tend to be happy with what they have. They usually have a positive outlook towards life and don't complain much. It doesn't mean that they don't have any problems. Of course, they have problems just like everyone else, but the difference between them and everyone else is that they can see the bigger picture and know that the challenges they are facing are a part of life. Maintaining a positive outlook towards life will provide you with the mental and the emotional strength that you will need for tackling any problem you come across. Remember that bad times will pass, and the right times are just around the corner. Don't lose hope in the meanwhile.

The ability to face reality is a sign of your mental and emotional strength. If you are going to overcome a hurdle or a challenge, then you should be able to tackle it head-on. Lying to yourself about your troubles won't make them go away, and you will just end up hurting yourself in the process. If you overeat when you are stressed or sad, accept the fact that there is a problem that needs to be addressed. Don't look for means of escape and try being honest with yourself.

Dealing with life

Whenever you feel that you are stuck in a difficult situation, take a while to think things through. Don't react instantly and don't be in a hurry to make a decision. It will provide you with sufficient time for your emotions to diffuse and you can start weighing in your options with an open mind. It is essential that you do this, regardless of the situation you are in. If you can afford to, then take some time and list down the pros and cons of a situation. Make a note of how you are feeling as well. Try finding some positive points about the situation you are in, and this can help to change your perspective towards things. At times, the smallest change in perception can make a huge difference. Follow the ten-second rule. Give yourself ten seconds for something to sink in before expressing yourself. Even if your partner tells you that he or she wants to end the relationship, take ten seconds to compose yourself and then respond.

Once you have managed to compose yourself, before you decide on the course of action, think clearly about the circumstance you are in. What happened and what are the possible options available to you? There will always be more than one path that you can opt for. For instance, let us assume that your friend asked you to do something morally wrong and you are torn between your loyalty to your friend and your sense of morality. So, now you will need to weigh the different pros and cons and decide accordingly.

Make use of your inner voice or your conscience to guide you. Trust your instincts, and you are likely to be correct. At times, the answer might be quite clear and distinct, but it may be hard to do the right thing. Do not let the problem fester into a more significant hassle than the one it already is. You need to take a call and stick to it. You can always ask others for an opinion and weigh their opinions before concluding. However, remember that it needs to be your own decision and no one else's. If you feel like you are stuck, think about what someone you admire would do in such a situation. The decision that you take should be something that you can live with. And don't do something because someone thinks that it is a good idea. Do it because you want to.

Reflect on your experiences

Once a problematic situation passes you by, think about the way in which you dealt with it and the outcome of that case. Would you like to change something about the way you dealt with it or are you proud of yourself? Remember that wisdom is derived from practice. Examining what happened and the way you dealt with it will help you to make any changes the next time you have to deal with a similar situation. If things worked out for you, then it is all good. However, if things didn't exactly go as you planned, even that's all right. You had a chance to learn, and that's what it was. It was a learning experience, and you will be careful in future.

Wanting not winning

If you want to become a winner, then you need to develop a "whatever it takes to get there" attitude. You need to be able to make tough decisions, pay the price, and overcome any difficulties you face on your road to victory. Before you start, you should ask yourself if you are willing to do all that it takes to achieve your goals. Without this level of dedication and commitment, you will not get very far in life.

It will not be easy

Achieving your goals will not be a cakewalk, so don't have any misconceptions about the hard work and effort it takes. Most people think it will be easy and when an obstacle crops up, they try to escape. Understand that there will be days when everything seems to be going your way and then there will days when nothing seems to be going your way. You cannot control the external factors, and all that you can do is handle the manner in which you react. Always have a plan in place and keep motoring forward. If you aren't ready to face any difficulties that come your way, it is unlikely that you will achieve success.

Focus on the reason

Ask yourself the reason why you want to achieve your goal. The intensity of what you feel will determine whether you will pursue it or not. For a while, instead of concentrating on how you want to achieve the goal, think about the reason.

Details matter

A significant reason why people don't follow their goals is that they aren't sure about what they are trying to achieve. You must be sure of what you are trying to achieve, make the description as detailed as you possibly can, and then commit yourself towards working on it. Your goal shouldn't be "I want to lose weight," work on making it detailed instead. A specific goal would be "I want to lose 15 pounds within three months." When your goal is this detailed, you know what you are supposed to do. A specific target helps you in coming up with a particular plan of action that will help in guiding you.

No negative thinking

Positive mental attitude can make all the difference in life. Positive self-talk is one of the best tools for toughening yourself up mentally. The words you say and think play a significant role in your life. You are capable of achieving anything you put your mind to as long as you believe in yourself. Usually, we concentrate so much on all the negative talk in life that we forget to look for the silver lining. The goals that happen to be the most important to you are the ones that are quite difficult, and all this leads to a lot of negative self-talk and self-doubt. Start to consciously monitor everything you say to yourself and others as well.

Make a vision board

You can find all the motivation you need to work towards a goal by creating a vision board. If you are thinking about losing all those extra pounds, then you should make a vision board that's full of pictures of fit people, and encouraging quotes. Place your vision board in a location that's visible, and it will help to reinforce your subconscious to work towards that goal as well.

Accountability matters

A significant obstacle that most people have is the lack of accountability or even a support system. You need a support system in place to keep you going even when you don't feel like. Establish your goals and discuss them with your partner. Your support buddy will help in increasing your accountability. You can also find someone who has accomplished something that you are trying to do, and you can seek guidance from such a person.

Write it all down

Make a note of all the things you want to achieve, the stage you are at present, and the destination you have in mind. You can set a time frame that suits your requirements. Write it down and keep reading it daily. You are training your subconscious to focus on your goals by doing this. It will help in making sure that you are on the right track.

Stop thinking about others

You need to believe in your goals, and it doesn't matter what others think. You shouldn't seek approval from others and should instead work on improving yourself. Stop wasting your time thinking about what others will think. Instead, focus all your energy on doing things that you think are significant. You should remember that what might be a good fit for you might not be for others. Start living your life the way you want to and not like someone else does.

Discipline matters

All those who are successful in life are quite disciplined. Discipline makes all the difference between right and great. The ability to stay on track and maintain your focus is quintessential. Keep pushing yourself regardless of whether you want to do something, or you don't. Don't get tempted by temporary gratification and instead focus on long-term satisfaction. Usually, we tend to avoid things that we think are difficult or painful. However, without overcoming difficulties, you will never be able to reach your goals.

Living in the present

Stop living in your past. If you have made any mistakes in the past, think of them as learning experiences and nothing else. Learn from your mistakes, prepare for your future, and live in the present. You cannot create a better future for yourself if you cannot let go of your past. Be oriented towards your future and your dreams. Keep going until you have reached those goals. If you are mentally strong, you can transform all your dreams into reality.

Chapter Five: Controlling Your Thoughts

More often than not, we tend to find that our minds are flooded with a lot of negative thoughts. These negative feelings can become quite powerful when you keep thinking about them endlessly. The problem starts when you start focusing on these thoughts, and they naturally become more powerful. Doing this makes it quite difficult to break free of the mental rut you may be in. In this chapter, you will learn about a couple of simple things that you can for controlling your thoughts.

Making a conscious decision

The problem is that, at times, we get attached to specific ideas and complications, and we subconsciously derive some weird form of pleasure from going through those issues. If you keep inviting such negative thoughts subconsciously, you will never be able to stop thinking about them. Therefore, the first step is to make a conscious decision to clear your mind and stop your mind from replaying all the negative thoughts on a constant loop. Be aware of the impact these negative thoughts have on you and prevent them from getting stuck in your mind. You need to make a conscious effort to stop all the negative thoughts from dwelling in your mind.

Separate your thoughts

When you try to stop individual views, you will notice that it seems incredibly difficult. It happens because ideas are a significant part of your mental process. The second stage is to separate yourself from your thoughts. Whenever a thought pops into your head, view them as if they are from an external source. It will help in reducing the impact negative thoughts have on your mind. Once you realize that you can, in fact, make this distinction, you can start modulating the ideas you think about. You should be able to control your thoughts, and it shouldn't be the other way around.

Who is thinking those thoughts?

You need to understand where your thoughts originate. Whenever an idea comes to you, first try to understand the reason why you are thinking that specific view. You need to realize that your thoughts can be controlled. Whenever it is a negative thought that's coming into your head, try diverting your attention towards something positive. If you find that you aren't able to do this, then try thinking about the cause of such a thought.

Conclusion

I would like to thank you once again for purchasing this book. I hope it proved to be an informative read.

You don't have to wait for a miracle to turn your life around. You don't need a genie to grant you something that you have wished for. By developing a simple trait, you can achieve everything that you have ever dreamt of. It isn't difficult, and the key to changing your life lies in your hands, and it is self-discipline.

In this book, you learned about the different steps that you can follow for developing self-discipline, found tips for improving self-confidence, controlling your thoughts and making yourself mentally tough enough to achieve your goals. All that you need is follow the simple steps and tips mentioned in this book, put in a little effort and show some patience. After a while, you will be able to see positive results.

Thank you and all the best!

Resources

https://www.inc.com/jeff-haden/7-habits-of-people-with-remarkable-mental-toughness.html

https://www.inc.com/peter-economy/5-powerful-ways-to-boost-your-confidence.html

https://www.entrepreneur.com/slideshow/299836

http://www.uncommonhelp.me/articles/self-discipline-techniques/

http://blog.iqmatrix.com/self-discipline

Made in the USA
San Bernardino, CA
26 July 2018